GARDENING WITH GRANDPA

Written by Khristine Griffin
Illustrated by Kelsey McSweeney

To order additional copies of this book, contact:
Xlibris
844-714-8691
www.Xlibris.com
Orders@Xlibris.com

ISBN: Softcover   978-1-6641-5836-8
       Hardcover   978-1-6641-5837-5
       EBook   978-1-6641-5835-1

Print information available on the last page

Rev. date: 02/19/2021

Gardening
with
Grandpa

This is a story about my grandpa and me.
It starts off with candy
but ends with a tree.

Does this sound like a mystery
that's got you all hooked?
Then keep on reading until
the end of the book.

Grandpa's day starts with a hot cup of Joe
and I tell him it's time and
we really must go.

I'll throw on my boots and run with a hop
right out the door so we can
start sowing our crop.

I ask him what seeds we are trying to grow,
he tells me squash and some
onions and red tomatoes.

We have lettuce and peppers
to get into the land
so we can sell them to neighbors
and friends from our stand.

We both have our jobs, you see, for our goal
I drop in the seed after he digs the hole.

We walk down the rows of
straight parallel lines
to cover them up and get
them watered in time.

It's just me and him in the heat of the day
spending time with each other,
with play in the way.

My mind starts to wander of
what else I should know
if I plants jellybeans, will a lollypop grow?

I ask grandpa his thoughts
and he says with a look
he said nothing will happen as
his head made a shook.

But what if I wished really
hard for my treat?
I know I'd give grandpa
the first one to eat.

The next morning came and
I ran out the door
and I couldn't believe it, my
mouth dropped to the floor.

There was my first lolly popped
out of the ground
I looked and I looked and they're all around.

So I ran in the house and
remembered a box
of old chocolate chips that
smelled like old sox.

I would throw them away if
it weren't for the trees
that I really must grow for
some yummy cookies.

So Grandpa started thinking
just like an adult,
he snuck out at night with
an expected result.

A bag of coins and some soil and water
we woke up at sunrise with
a tree full of dollars.

The neighbors all gathered
around in the sun
but I liked my cookies, the tree was no fun.

It took him away from our fun that we have
when we're out in the
garden, him in his hat.

He scooped me up tight
and said with a smile,
you're right about that, your
treats win by a mile.

We went back to our garden
and finished the day
just me and my grandpa enjoying the play.

Printed in the United States
by Baker & Taylor Publisher Services